Secrets of Shred Guitar

by Dave Celentano

Cover design by Design Associates

ISBN-13: 978-157424-218-8
ISBN-10: 1-57424-218-0
SAN 683-8022

CENTERSTREAM

Audio CD Track List

Contents

Introduction

This book introduces the guitarist to many of the techniques used in the style of shred including sweep picking, alternate picking, string skipping, multi-finger tapping, legato, trills, and tremolo picking. These techniques are broken down into a series of exercises and melodic etudes. The exercises and melodic etudes are arranged in order of difficulty from easiest to most challenging, and each concentrates on and develops a specific skill. The accompanying audio CD features the exercises and melodic etudes played at normal and slow tempos. The first section includes six short exercises - three focusing on the picking hand and three working the fret hand. These are followed by sixteen melodic etudes written in the 'neo-classical' style where the author combined elements of shred guitar and classical music. For the advanced guitarist the melodic etudes can be used as daily warm-ups to keep the chops in shape.

The Recording

The audio CD was recorded at Yaking Cat Music Studios

Dave Celentano - all guitars

Brandon Amison - engineer

Acknowledgments

Ben Cole at GHS strings and Rocktron, Lowe's Music, and all my students (past, present, and future).

How To Practice

First, play through the entire piece slowly to get a feel for position changes and awkward areas. Next, learn and memorize one measure at a time. Only when the fingering and picking are mastered is one to move on to the second measure. Economy of motion can not be over stressed. Both hands should make the smallest motions possible at all times. For speed picking the pick should strike the string with the very tip, making small down and up strokes. Small motions = speed. Take this challenge - while alternate picking on one string, don't let the pick go further than one sixteenth of an inch past the string in either direction. Pretty tough, huh. The back and forth motion of the picking hand should come from the wrist, not the elbow or forearm. As for the fret hand fingers - when not used they should float in idle position just above the fret board rather than flailing about uncontrolled. Generally, both hands should be as relaxed as possible.

Most importantly, practice everything in this book with a metronome and keep a log of current tempos for each exercise. The metronome tempo indications for the exercises are just suggestions. A piece can be played faster, of course, but only when it's perfected at a slower tempo first.

Anytime a phrase or passage causes one to 'stumble', stop and back up to just before the trouble spot. From this point move *slowly* forward, playing through the tricky area to a few notes just beyond. Repeat this 'micro exercise' several times slowly until the fingers are comfortable and can perform with no interruptions. Isolating small portions and diligently (and patiently!!) working through each is one of the best ways to master the guitar.

Explanation of Musical Terms and Symbols

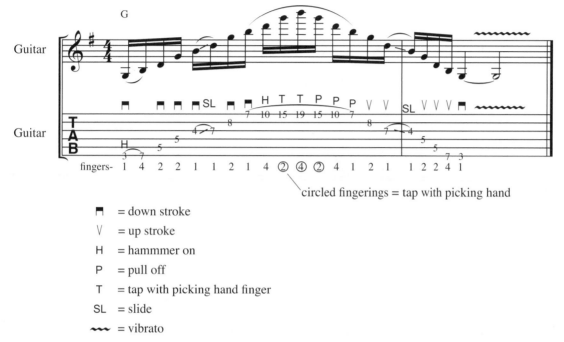

circled fingerings = tap with picking hand

⊓ = down stroke

V = up stroke

H = hammmer on

P = pull off

T = tap with picking hand finger

SL = slide

〰 = vibrato

simile = continue with same pattern

Tuning Notes

All the exercises are tuned to A 440. Track three on the audio CD gives the correct tuning pitches for the six open strings. Listen to one string at a time from the CD, pausing after each to tune the corresponding string.

Exercise 1

A great way to increase the speed of the picking hand is to work with short 'speed bursts', then gradually work up to longer groups. The idea is to play a repeating set of notes slowly (at half speed), then without stopping, increase to full speed, followed by a return to the slower tempo. This is repeated two more times culminating in a longer full speed burst. Find a tempo slow enough on the metronome that one can perform the exercise with no breaks. Since each string is of varying thickness and feels different under the pick, the student is encouraged to transpose this and the next two exercises to the remaining five strings.

Track #4

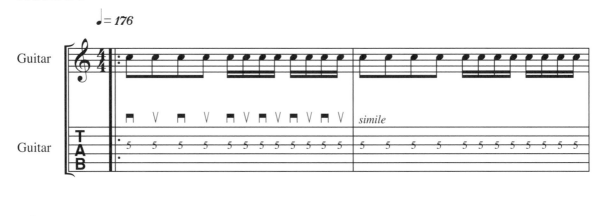

Exercise 2

Here's a cool classical style melody that employs 'tremolo picking'. Tremolo is the rapid repetition of a single note that creates the illusion of a sustained note. Pickers will find a steady down-up-down-up pick stroke works best. Start out slow while *listening* for smoothness of notes - equal volume and duration. Repeat this exercise on the remaining five strings.

Track #6

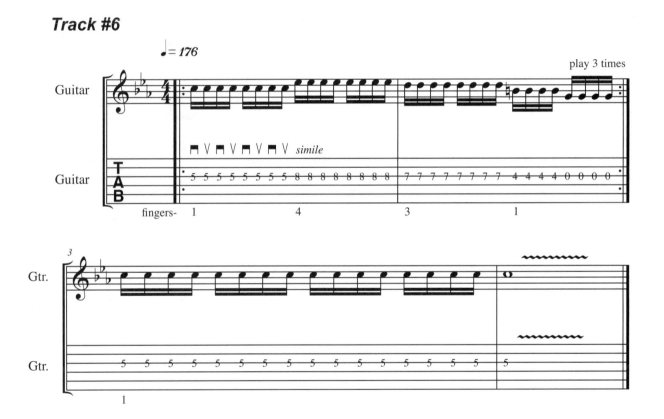

<u>Exercise 3</u>

Exercise 3 is adapted from a section of J.S. Bach's "Toccata and Fugue" in D minor, but here it's transposed to C minor. This author also incorporated tremolo picking on the open third string (G) in between the melody notes. This type of tremolo where the first sixteenth note is the melody and the following three sixteenths are the repeated pedal is used by classical guitarists (who, by the way, use a picking hand combination of thumb, ring, middle, and index fingers to perform tremolo). Begin by memorizing the fret hand positions, then slow and steadily play along with a metronome. And finally, apply this to the remaining five strings.

Track #8

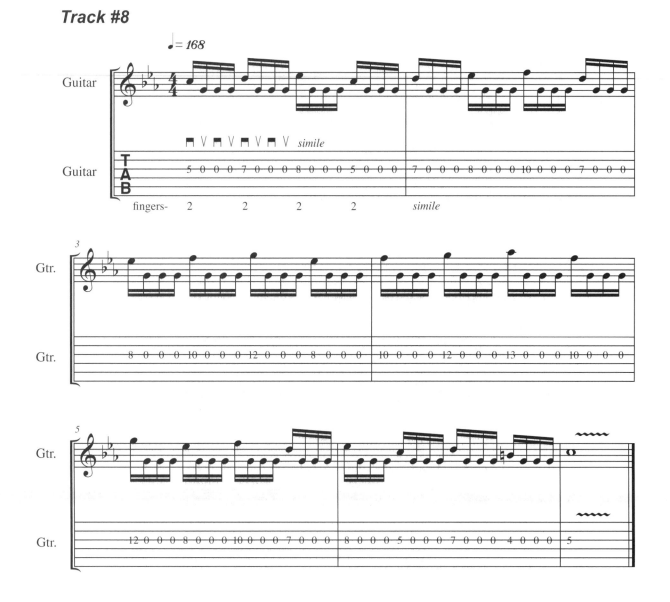

Exercise 4

Trills are a great way to warm up the fret hand fingers and exercises 4, 5, and 6 use short trills moving across all six strings. A trill is a series of rapidly repeating hammer ons and pull offs. Each series begins with a down stroke followed by hammer on - pull off - hammer on. Some players may find the transition to the next string challenging to perform clean, so take the first two series (eight notes) and repeat them slowly back and forth. This should be performed as smooth as possible with no breaks. Exercise 4 works fingers one and two, while exercises 5 and 6 employ fingers one and three, and one and four respectively.

Track #10

Exercise 5

Track #12

<u>*Exercise 6*</u>

Track #14

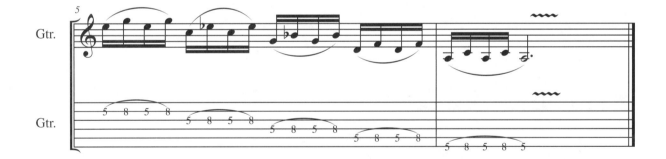

11

Melodic Etudes

The sixteen melodic etudes were written over a classical style chord progression. The first half - Am/ E7/ Am/ E7 - is repeated, then the second section launches into a cycle of fourths in A minor - A/ Dm/ G/ C/ F/ B dim/ E7/ Am - eventually coming full circle back to the tonic 'Am'. In a cycle of fourths each chord is four scale degrees higher than it's predecessor and the chords stay primarily diatonic. The two exceptions are the first chord 'A', which has been temporarily altered from minor to major, elevating the mood with it's happy sonority, and the seventh chord 'E7' which implies the A harmonic minor scale. The final two chords - E7/ Am (V chord to I chord) - produce a cadence that instills a sense of final resolution and is used in many styles of music including classical, jazz, and blues. In music theory this is referred to as a V (dominant) to I (tonic) cadence.

The melody note choices where determined by the chord assigned to that measure. In other words the individual chord tones are the frame work for writing the melodies, although not all chord tones are required to imply a chord. For instance, ideas over E7 often use the E triad (E,G#,B) as in melodic etudes 11, 12, and 15, meanwhile, melodic etudes 1, 3, and 9 include all the notes of E7 (E,G#,B,D). Some even combine chord tones with occasional 'neighboring' scale tones (melodic etudes 2, 5, 7, and 8).

Melodic Etude 1

Technique developed - 'alternate picking'

Your fingers will be traversing the fret board in no time with this playful etude in 2/4. It begins with a four measure melody repeated one octave higher at measures 5-8, then gradually descends to the original starting position. Notice each note is picked twice and alternate picking should be employed (pay attention to the pick stroke directions above the tablature). Randy Rhoads used double picking like this to build a fast and exciting ascending run during his solo in "I Don't Know" from Ozzy Osbourne's 'Blizzard of Ozz' album. For extra credit try picking each note four times.

Melodic Etude 1

by Dave Celentano

Melodic Etude 2

Techniques developed - 'pedal point' and 'alternate picking'

Bach inspired this etude which utilizes a two note pedal point device. By definition a pedal point is a note(s) that is held while other notes move above or below. Here the pedal point is a three note grouping of two notes that shuttle back and forth. They occur as the last three notes of every four sixteenth notes while the melody notes change on the first of the four sixteenth notes. A little confused? Play through the first measure to here this in action.

Try breaking down the first measure into four separate 'micro exercises', making each beat of four sixteenth notes one exercise that repeats several times. Note: the second and fourth beats are actually the same. Apply this micro exercise routine to every measure. In fact, put this to use with all the melodic etudes in this book.

Melodic Etude 2

Track #18

by Dave Celentano

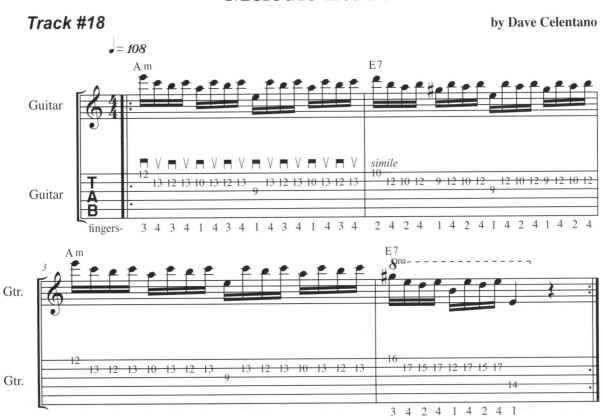

Melodic Etude 2 continued

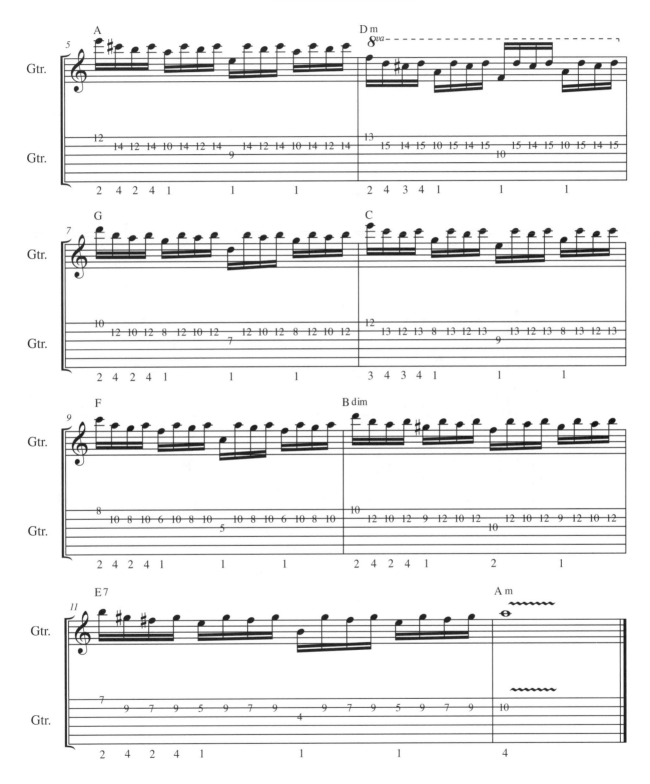

Melodic Etude 3

Techniques developed - 'string skipping' and 'alternate picking'

Here we'll explore string skipping using violin style arpeggios. Economy of motion is required of the picking hand and to achieve speed the pick must move no more than an eighth inch (preferably less) past the string after being struck in either direction (the faster one picks the smaller this distance must be). All this skipping action takes place between the G and high E strings. Begin by repeating just the first measure slowly and watch the picking hand, making the smallest motions possible to strike the strings.

Melodic Etude 3

Track #20

by Dave Celentano

Melodic Etude 4

Techniques developed - 'string skipping', 'alternate picking', and 'pedal point'

This etude uses a single pedal point that trades back and forth with descending and ascending chord tones. As the piece progresses the string skips gradually expand and contract. Notice the pick stroke directions use 'outside picking'. This is where each pick stroke sends the pick in the direction of the next string. To see this in action play measure 1 slowly, adhering to the pick indications, and watch the picking hand.

Melodic Etude 4

Track #22

by Dave Celentano

Melodic Etude 5

Techniques developed - 'alternate picking', 'string skipping', 'pull off', and 'hammer on'

Bach's second son, Karl Philipp Emanuel Bach, originally wrote 'Solfeggietto' in C minor. For melodic etude 5 this author borrowed the first twelve measures, transposed it to A minor, and added the last four measures.

The first eight measures ascend the fret board rather quickly utilizing several position shifts, which must be performed with grace. Turn each measure with a position shift into a 'micro exercise'. These measures are: 1, 2, 3, 5, and 7. Begin by playing slow through the first measure, then stop briefly to analyze for smoothness during the shift. There should be no hesitation when the shift occurs. Keep an eye on the first finger (index) as it bars across the fourth and fifth notes during the five measures containing the shifts. The four micro exercises below should be repeated until the shift is comfortable.

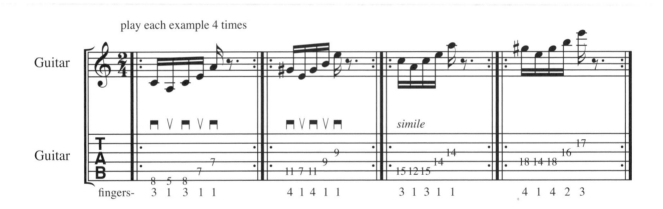

The arpeggios in the latter half (measures 9 - 11) use string skipping and several wide stretches often associated with Paul Gilbert's shred style. Start slow at first by learning one measure at a time and keep a steady beat. Pay close attention to the pick directions and mute strings not being used with the heel/palm of the picking hand. Sympathetic string noise seems to be a problem here and the challenge is to reduce it as much as possible. In fact, a slight bit of palm muting used during the entire piece will help clean it up.

Melodic Etude 5

Track #24

by Karl Philipp Emanuel Bach

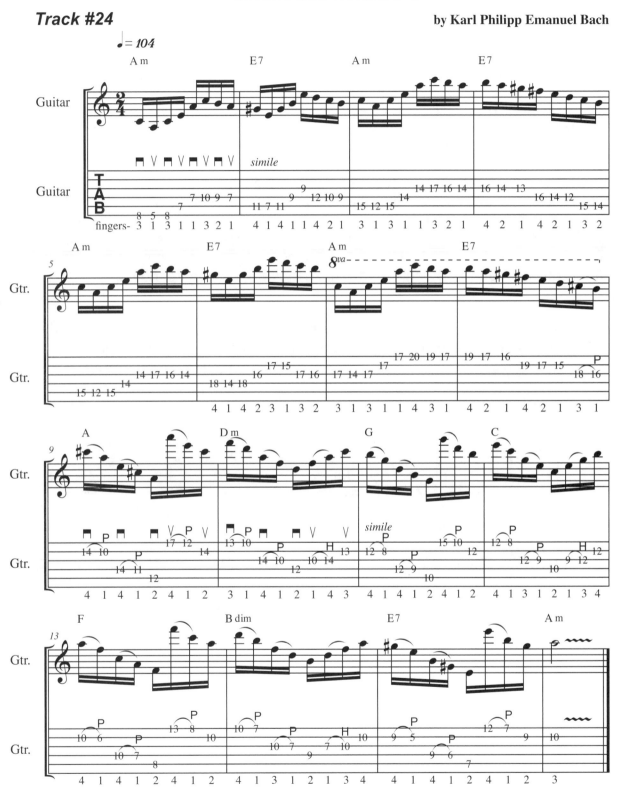

Melodic Etude 6

Techniques developed - 'pull off' and 'alternate picking'

Inspired by the intro to Randy Rhoads' second solo in 'Mr. Crowley', this etude flies over the changes with a rapid fire triplet arpeggio figure. Notice the picking sequence is up-down with a pull off sandwiched in between. Try leaving the first finger anchored on the first string to help with speed. The solo from the Eagles' classic 'Hotel California' begins with triplet arpeggios played in a similar fashion.

'Voice leading' is used for the ascending triads in the second half. This is where each chord contains one note in common with the next chord - A major (A, C#, E) to D minor (D, F, A) have the 'A' note in common, while D minor (D, F, A) to G major (G, B, D) share the 'D' note, etc. Try learning the note names for all these triad shapes and write the answers just above the notes in this book. By doing this exercise with the other melodic etudes one will eventually begin to memorize the notes on the fret board.

For a variation on this etude transpose the entire piece down one octave. Here's what to do: move the same arpeggio 'shapes' from the top two strings (E and B) down to the two middle strings (G and D) and shift back three frets. See the example below.

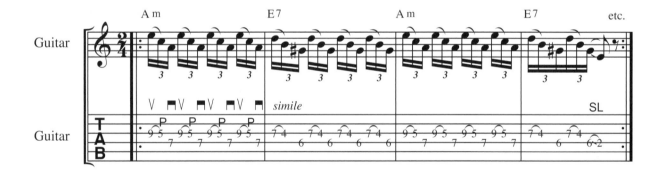

20

Melodic Etude 6

Track #26

by Dave Celentano

Melodic Etude 7

Techniques developed - 'pull off' and 'hammer on'

Melodic etude 7 uses 'legato' technique with a series of pull offs and hammer ons. By definition legato means to perform with a smooth and even tone, without breaks between the notes. Here, the first note of every six is picked with a down stroke, while the remaining five notes are generated by a pull off or hammer on. This is a great workout and strength builder for all fingers involved, especially the pinkie.

A proper pull off is achieved by pulling the finger off the string in a downward manner - in essence plucking the string. A correct hammer on is done by the finger striking the string with a little force from just above the fret board (perpendicular) - like a hammer tapping a nail into a surface.

While playing listen for and eliminate all unwanted string noise. Most of the time this comes from the strings one is _not_ playing. The natural vibrations from the guitar cause strings to softly vibrate producing the sympathetic noise. Reduce this by muting the four bass strings (E, A, D, and G) with the heel/palm of the pick hand lightly resting on these strings near the bridge.

Legato technique requires strong fret hand fingers and below are two exercises to fortify those digits.

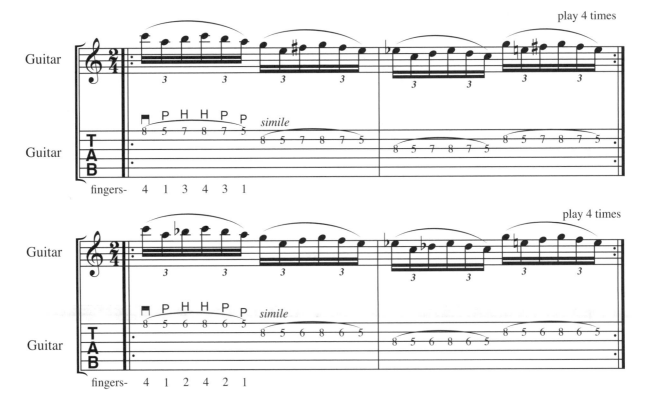

Melodic Etude 7

Track #28

by Dave Celentano

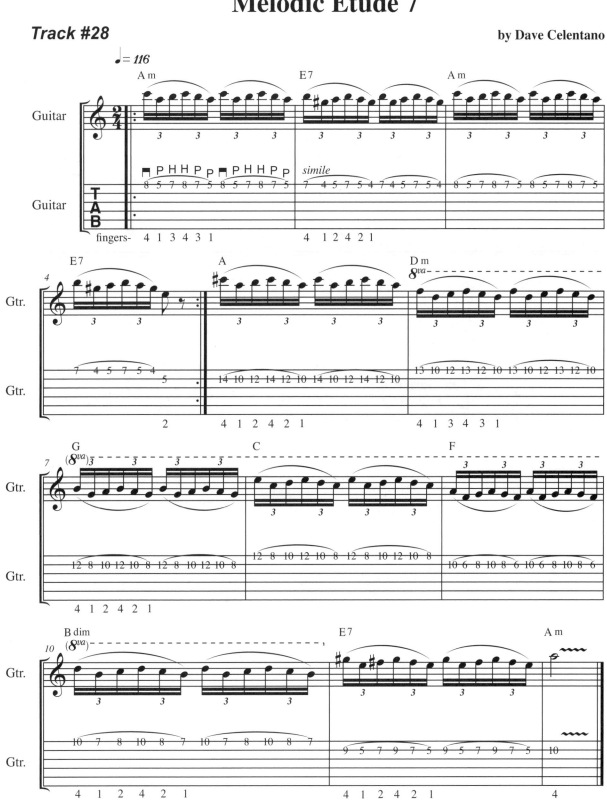

Melodic Etude 8

Techniques developed - 'hammer on', 'pull off', and 'position shift'

Here's an adaptation of violinist Niccolo Paganini's '24th Caprice (variation 7)' with the last four measures adjusted to fit the established chord progression of the previous melodic etudes. While performing the hammer ons and pull offs aim for a smooth and steady tone where all notes are the same volume. The most challenging aspects are the position shifts, which are abundant. Begin by locating the measures with a position shift and turn each into a 'micro exercise' by repeating several times *slowly* until the transition feels comfortable and is seamless to the ear.

Manage the sympathetic string noise by palm muting slightly with the picking hand. Watch out for measures 5-11 as they tend to get crazy with the noise factor.

Below is a great exercise for developing the rapid hammers and pulls required for this etude. Rapidly repeating two notes in an alternating manner like this is called a 'trill'. The objective is to keep a steady trill and change strings without hesitation.

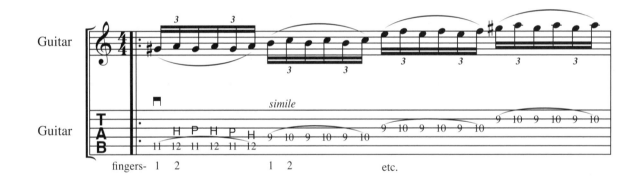

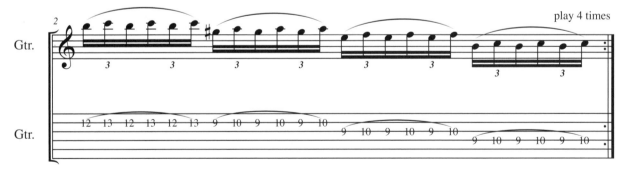

Melodic Etude 8

Track #30

by Niccolo Paganini

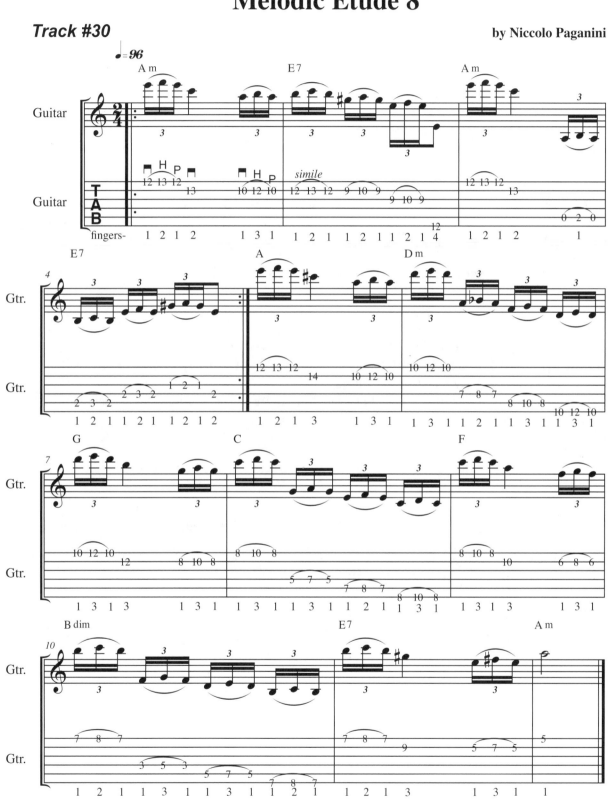

Melodic Etude 9

Techniques developed - 'sweep picking', hammer on', 'pull off', and 'position shift'

These three string triad arpeggio shapes combine sweep picking, hammer ons, and pull offs to produce a liquid texture. The essence of sweep picking is to keep the pick moving in the same direction for two or more notes on consecutive strings. Check this out during the third and fourth notes and eighth through tenth using two and three string down sweeps respectively.

During the sweep it's important to _not_ let the notes sustain over each other - as the next note is struck the previous note is stopped by slightly releasing pressure from the string. Practice this move slowly and repeat several times.

The picking hand should make _one continuous down motion_ plowing through the strings involving the sweep rather than making a separate pick stroke for each string. Think of the sweep motion as one slow motion down strum (or up strum) like when strumming a chord.

Break the first measures twelve note sequence into two halves and play the first six notes several times by making a continuous repeating loop. Next, follow the same procedure with the second half. Always begin by playing slowly and steadily without hesitations. The two examples below illustrate this exercise.

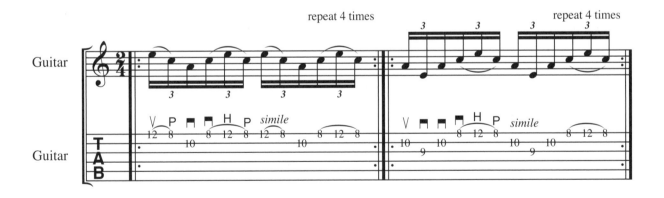

Melodic Etude 9

Track #32

by Dave Celentano

Melodic Etude 10

Techniques developed - 'sweep picking' and 'hammer on'

This three string sweep etude develops the 'up sweep'. Make sure the pick makes one continuous upward motion, rather than three separate up strokes. When performing a sweep the pick should come to rest immediately on the next string poised and ready for action. This is similar to the 'rest stroke' used by classical guitarists.

Typically shred style guitarists play with a good amount of gain which can cause additional string noise if not harnessed and controlled. Avoid the unpleasant sound of two notes sounding together by letting each note sustain just up to the next without overlapping.

In measure 2 (and several other measures) the second finger is required to play three consecutive notes on two neighboring strings (D and G). The finger should barre both strings, but make a slight rolling motion from one to the next as they are picked. This move requires a bit of coordination from the knuckle nearest the tip of the 2nd finger, but once mastered, will minimize some of the string noise.

Practice the up sweep by repeating the exercise below slowly and steadily:

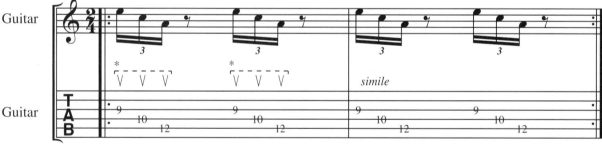

* = one continuous up stroke

Melodic Etude 10

Track #34

by Dave Celentano

Melodic Etude 11

Techniques developed - 'sweep picking', 'pull off', 'hammer on', and 'position shift'

Melodic etude 11 combines five string arpeggio sweeps with rapid position shifts. The picking hand motion for the big sweeps can be compared to strumming - make one big continuous upward motion by pushing the pick through the five strings involved, then follow with a big down motion. The idea is to keep the pick moving smoothly, with no hesitations, as it cuts across the strings. While performing slow, pick the first up stroke and bring the pick to rest on the underside of the second string during the pull off, then follow through coming to rest on each subsequent string until the final up stroke. Repeat this 'resting' technique in the opposite direction for the five down strokes.

After every six notes the fretting hand makes a swift position change jumping as many as eight frets. The transitions between arpeggio shapes must be seamless, and the best way to nail this is to work with two consecutive arpeggios at a time. Begin with the first measure and slowly repeat until the two arpeggios can be performed without hesitation.

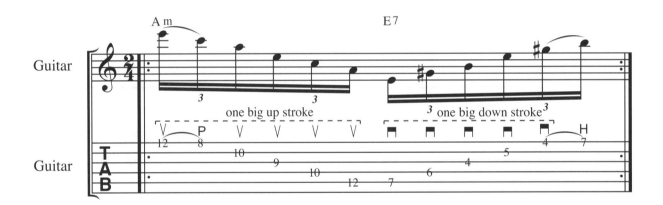

Practice with a metronome and keep a log of current tempos for all the melodic etudes.

Melodic Etude 11

Track #36

by Dave Celentano

Melodic Etude 12

Techniques developed - 'sweep picking', 'pull off', 'hammer on', and 'position shift'

This sweep picking etude merges the three and five string arpeggio shapes from the two previous etudes in a frenzy of notes. The objective is to achieve a 'liquid' tone, like water effortlessly flowing down a windy river. Here's two important points regarding this:

1.) Connect the notes, but don't let any overlap - stop one just as the next is struck. When using gain (distortion, over drive, fuzz, etc.), overlapping notes tend to create dissonant overtones. Remember, an arpeggio is a broken chord - a chord whose notes are played consecutively instead of together.

2.) Make smooth and graceful transitions when shifting positions from one arpeggio to another.

Begin by rehearsing the first two measures until consistent evenness is achieved.

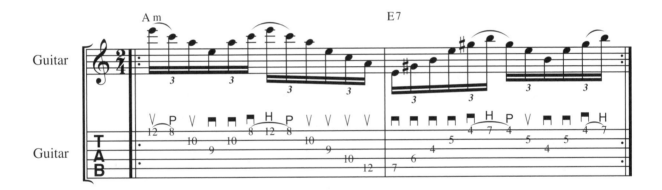

Melodic Etude 12

by Dave Celentano

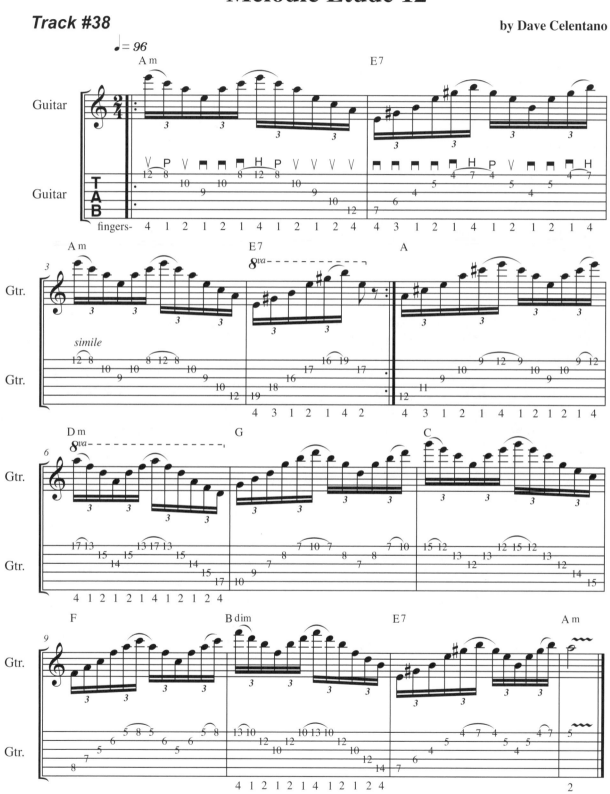

Melodic Etude 13

Techniques developed - 'single finger tapping', pull off', and 'hammer on'

Here's a cool idea right from the Edward Van Halen school of tapping. Similar to the tapping arpeggios that conclude his masterpiece 'Eruption', these also follow a classical chord progression by playing the chords arpeggio style. Tapping is the act of hammering on a note with a finger from the picking hand and usually following with a pull off to a lower note (held by a fret hand finger) on the same string.

A few tips on tapping:

1.) Anchor the tapping hand thumb on the top edge of the guitar neck for support.

2.) The tap finger should strike the string from directly above - perpendicular to the fret board.

3.) When pulling off from a tapped note, the tap finger should pull the string in an up-ward motion. Note: this could also be achieved by 'pushing' the tap finger off in a downward motion. One should attempt both and decide which is easier *and* produces the cleanest tone (least string noise).

The latter half (measures 5 - 12) employs 'voice leading' which uses one common note to transition to the next chord - A to Dm have the 'A' note in common, Dm to G share 'D', etc. The student should find the common notes for the remaining pairs of chords.

Notice the entire piece is performed on the 'B' string. For additional fun use the same fret numbers, but move over to the 'G' string (or any other string). This results in a key change to 'F minor'. Illustrated below are the first two measures transposed the the 'G' string in F minor.

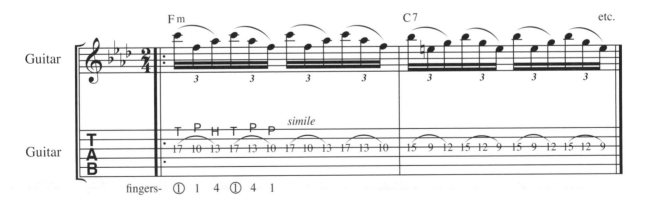

Melodic Etude 13

Track #40

by Dave Celentano

Melodic Etude 14

Techniques developed - 'single finger tapping', 'pull off', and 'hammer on'

The first half of this roller coaster tapping sequence begins like the previous, but then pulls off to the open string, followed by a series of ascending hammers and descending pull offs. This is a delight to play, but a few of the stretches may prove challenging (measures 9 and 11). Every note in each sequence is a chord tone - even the open string which is the same note as the twelfth fret tap, but one octave lower.

This etude develops tapping on the lower strings which may be difficult at first. Ease into the thicker strings by practicing the sequence on a thinner string. Below are the first four measures transposed to the 'B' string with the resulting key change being E minor.

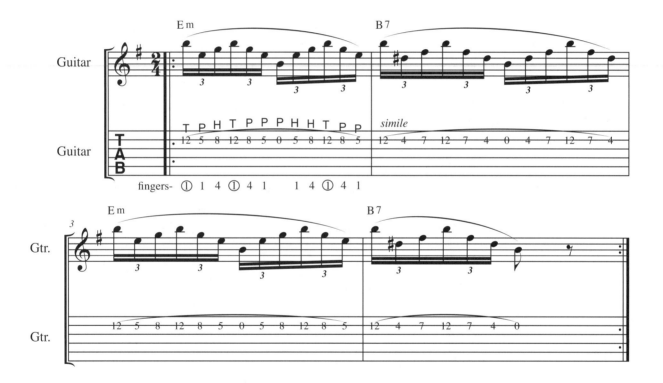

Melodic Etude 14

Track #42

by Dave Celentano

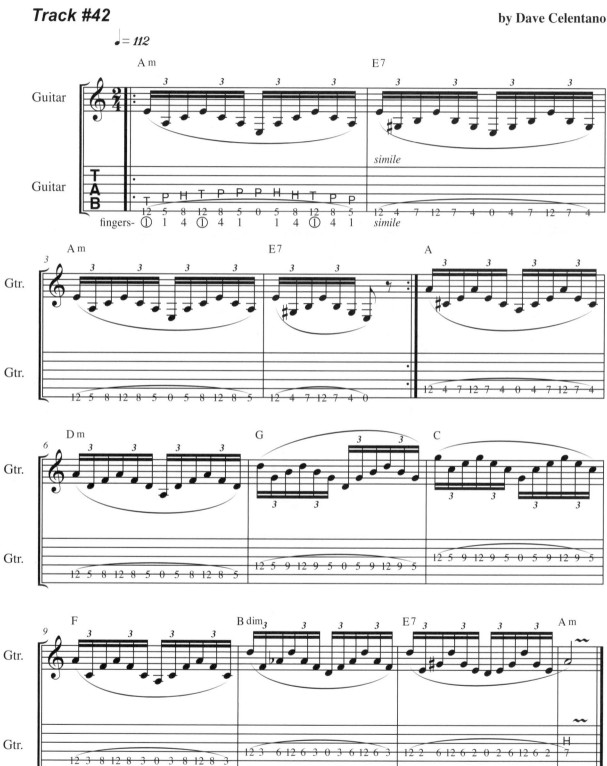

Melodic Etude 15

Techniques developed - 'multi-finger tapping', 'pull off', and 'hammer on'

Melodic etude 15 is a challenging multi-finger tap sequence that playfully ascends and descends on one string, and introduces the fourth finger (pinkie). Break the sequence into four groups of three notes and begin by mastering the first group which involves the index and pinkie fingers of the tapping hand. Next, add the second group of three notes and rehearse as a six note group. Continue adding three more notes until the entire twelve note sequence is mastered. Anchor the thumb of the tapping hand on the top edge of the guitar neck for support while tapping. Also, pull offs from a tapped finger should make an upward motion.

When tapping, the fret hand first finger (index) has three functions:

1.) Fret the note at hand
2.) Mute the string above with the tip/flesh
3.) Mute the string below with the front of the finger (finger print side)

Use this muting technique to prevent undesired string noise.

Melodic Etude 15

Track #44

by Dave Celentano

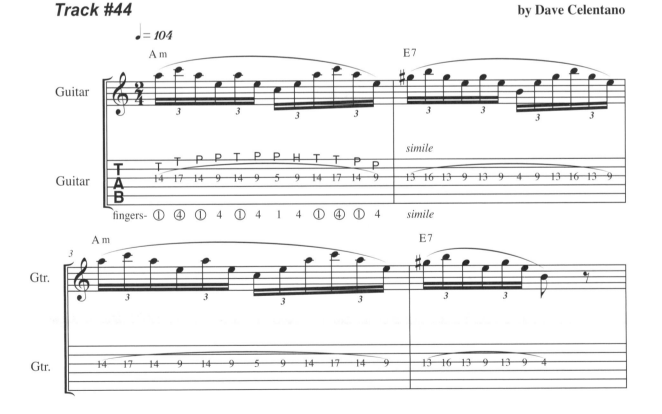

Melodic Etude 15 continued

39

Melodic Etude 16

Techniques developed - 'multi-finger tapping' and 'pull off'

Three tapping fingers and multiple strings are used in melodic etude 16. Here the two hands ping pong back and forth beginning with a tap and followed by a pull off to the fretting hand for every two notes. The first six notes of each measure establish the 'shape' and suggested fingering for the arpeggio sequence.

Each measure is a sixteen note sequence that can be broken down into three smaller sections of six, four, and six notes. Notice the last group is the same as the first. Learning pieces in small digestible chucks like this is one of the best ways to learn and master a song. Start with the first measure and learn the initial six notes to see the 'shape'. Next, add the following four notes to the first six and practice until it feels comfortable. And lastly, tag on the last six. Once the sequence is mastered learning the next measure is just a matter of changing frets.

Melodic Etude 16

Track #46

by Dave Celentano

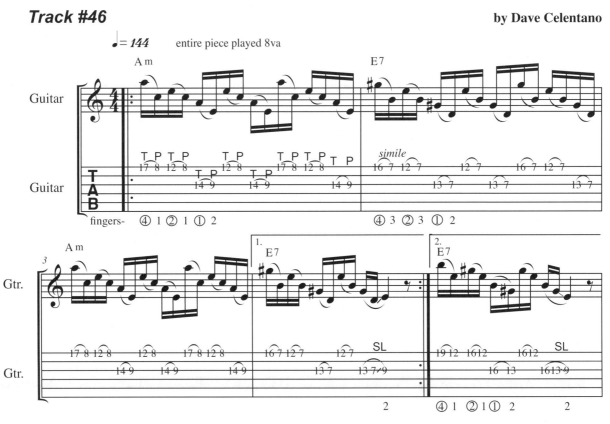

40

Melodic Etude 16 continued

Grand Finale

Grand Finale is the tapping piece featured at the introduction of the accompanying audio CD to this book. The piece follows the same chord changes as the previous sixteen melodic etudes, but with a slight twist - a transposition to 'E minor' (the original key was A minor). The first section (measures 1-4) bounces back and forth between Em and B7 on the 'B' string using the sequence from melodic etude 14. The next section switches to the sequence from melodic etude 13 and gradually ascends the fret board employing 'voice leading' through the end of the piece.

Measures 15 and 16 kick it up a notch by shifting to 32nd notes, which squeeze eight notes into every beat. The trilling effect in measure 16 is produced by tapping the 17th fret, followed by a pull off to the 12th fret. Next, the same 17th fret note is *hammered* by the fret hand fourth finger, then concludes with a pull off to the 12th fret. Repeat this sequence steadily with a metronome allowing no breaks during the trill. For the tap notes, pull the finger off with an upward motion and the hammer on notes pull off downward. This helps prevent the two fingers from colliding.

This is a great piece to perform on other strings as well. Move to another string and use the same frets and suggested fingerings. Below are the first four measures transposed to the to the third string (G).

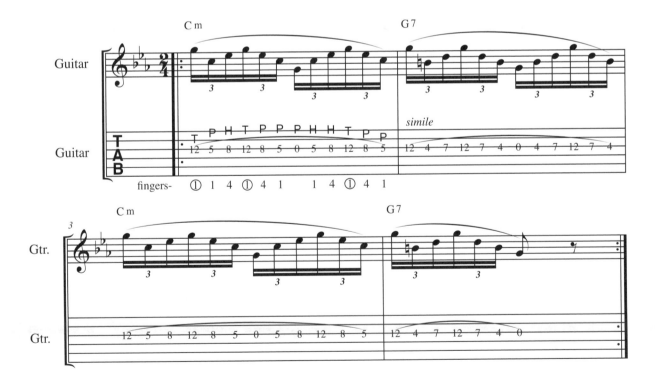

42

Grand Finale

Track #48

by Dave Celentano

Grand Finale continued

Conclusion

The sixteen melodic etudes were intended to serve as a launching platform to bring ones playing to new heights and broader directions. I hope that in the course of working through the etudes you've discovered a few new ideas and techniques. Along with using a metronome integrate these exercises in a daily practice routine. Remember, there are no short cuts - the only way to achieve monster shredder chops is through hard work and diligent practice.

- Dave Celentano

photo by Brandon Amison

About The Author

Dave Celentano is a sought after guitar instructor in the Los Angeles area and has been teaching for over 20 years. Along with educating students privately and in group classes, he's written and published over 30 books, videos, DVDs, and CDs (which can be found at *musicdispatch.com* or *davecelentano.com*) that instruct the student in a wide variety of styles including blues, surf guitar, neo-classical, heavy metal, and rock, and techniques like sweep picking, multi-finger tapping, and transcribing.

As an endorsee of GHS strings, Dave's shared his expertise and pedagogic chops with students during clinics at M.I.(Musician's Institute) and music stores throughout the south-west U.S.

Dave was featured in Guitar Player Magazine's 'Spotlight' column in May, 1991.

One of Dave's previous bands 'Sir Real' released a progressive rock CD in Japan in 1994.

Dave's latest CD "Guitar Stew" can be previewed and purchased through his web site listed below. Currently, he's recording new music for an upcoming CD of instrumental hard rock/shred.

Contact Dave at *DAVECELENTANO.COM* or write to:

Flying Fingers Music

P.O. Box 800036

Santa Clarita, CA 91380

GUITAR INSTRUCTION & TECHNIQUE

THE GUITAR CHORD SHAPES OF CHARLIE CHRISTIAN
Book/CD Pack
by Joe Weidlich
The concepts and fingerings in this book have been developed by analyzing the licks used by Charlie Christian. Chord shapes are moveable; thus one can play the riffs in virtually any key without difficulty by simply moving the shape, and fingerings used to play them, up or down the fingerboard. The author shows how the chord shapes – F, D and A – are formed, then can easily be modified to major, minor, dominant seventh and diminished seventh chord voicings.†Analyzing licks frequently used by Charlie Christian, Joe has identified a series of what he calls tetrafragments, i.e., the core element of a lick. The identifiable "sound" of a particular lick is preserved regardless of how many notes are added on either side of it, e.g., pickup notes or tag endings.† Many examples are shown and played on the CD of how this basic concept was used by Charlie Christian to keep his solo lines moving forward. Weidlich also makes observations on the physical manner Charlie Christian used in playing jazz guitar and how that approach contributed to his smooth, mostly down stroke, pick technique.
00000388 Guitar $19.95

GUITAR CHORDS PLUS
by Ron Middlebrook
A comprehensive study of normal and extended chords, tuning, keys, transposing, capo use, and more. Includes over 500 helpful photos and diagrams, a key to guitar symbols, and a glossary of guitar terms.
00000011 ....$11.95

GUITAR TRANSCRIBING – A COMPLETE GUIDE
by Dave Celentano
Learn that solo now! Don't wait for the music to come out – use this complete guide to writing down what you hear. Includes tips, advice, examples and exercises from easy to difficult. Your ear is the top priority and you'll train it to listen more effectively to recognize intervals, chords, note values, counting rhythms and much more for an accurate transcription.
00000378 Book/CD Pack $19.95

GUITAR TUNING FOR THE COMPLETE MUSICAL IDIOT (FOR SMART PEOPLE TOO)
by Ron Middlebrook
A complete book on how to tune up. Contents include: Everything You Need To Know About Tuning; Intonation; Strings; 12-String Tuning; Picks; and much more.
00000002 ....$5.95

INTRODUCTION TO ROOTS GUITAR
by Doug Cox
This book/CD pack by Canada's premier guitar and Dobro® player introduces beginning to intermediate players to many of the basics of folk/roots guitar. Topics covered include: basic theory, tuning, reading tablature, right- and left-hand patterns, blues rhythms, Travis picking, frailing patterns, flatpicking, open tunings, slide and many more. CD includes 40 demonstration tracks.
00000262 Book/CD Pack $17.95
00000265 VHS Video $19.95

KILLER PENTATONICS FOR GUITAR
by Dave Celentano
Covers innovative and diverse ways of playing pentatonic scales in blues, rock and heavy metal. The licks and ideas in this book will give you a fresh approach to playing the pentatonic scale, hopefully inspiring you to reach for higher levels in your playing. The 37-minute companion CD features recorded examples.
00000285 Book/CD Pack $17.95

LEFT HAND GUITAR CHORD CHART
by Ron Middlebrook
Printed on durable card stock, this "first-of-a-kind" guitar chord chart displays all forms of major and minor chords in two forms, beginner and advanced.
00000005 ....$2.95

MELODIC LINES FOR THE INTERMEDIATE GUITARIST
by Greg Cooper
This book/CD pack is essential for anyone interested in expanding melodic concepts on the guitar. Author Greg Cooper covers: picking exercises; major, minor, dominant and altered lines; blues and jazz turn-arounds; and more.
00000312 Book/CD Pack $19.95

MELODY CHORDS FOR GUITAR
by Allan Holdsworth
Influential fusion player Allan Holdsworth provides guitarists with a simplified method of learning chords, in diagram form, for playing accompaniments and for playing popular melodies in "chord-solo" style. Covers: major, minor, altered, dominant and diminished scale notes in chord form, with lots of helpful reference tables and diagrams.
00000222 ....$19.95

MODAL JAMS AND THEORY
by Dave Celentano
This book shows you how to play the modes, the theory behind mode construction, how to play any mode in any key, how to play the proper mode over a given chord progression, and how to write chord progressions for each of the seven modes. The CD includes two rhythm tracks and a short solo for each mode so guitarists can practice with a "real" band.
00000163 Book/CD Pack $17.95

MONSTER SCALES AND MODES
by Dave Celentano
This book is a complete compilation of scales, modes, exotic scales, and theory. It covers the most common and exotic scales, theory on how they're constructed, and practical applications. No prior music theory knowledge is necessary, since every section is broken down and explained very clearly.
00000140 ....$7.95

OLD TIME COUNTRY GUITAR BACKUP BASICS
by Joseph Weidlich
This instructional book uses commercial recordings from 70 different "sides" from the 1920s and early 1930s as its basis to learn the principal guitar backup techniques commonly used in old-time country music. Topics covered include: boom-chick patterns • bass runs • uses of the pentatonic scale • rhythmic variations • minor chromatic nuances • the use of chromatic passing tones • licks based on chords or chord progressions • and more.
00000389 ....$15.95

OPEN GUITAR TUNINGS
by Ron Middlebrook
This booklet illustrates over 75 different tunings in easy-to-read diagrams. Includes tunings used by artists such as Chet Atkins, Michael Hedges, Jimmy Page, Joe Satriani and more for rock, blues, bluegrass, folk and country styles including open D (for slide guitar), Em, open C, modal tunings and many more.
00000130 ....$4.95

OPEN TUNINGS FOR GUITAR
by Dorian Michael
This book provides 14 folk songs in 9 tunings to help guitarists become comfortable with changing tunings. Songs are ordered so that changing from one tuning to another is logical and non-intrusive. Includes: Fisher Blues (DADGBE) • Fine Toast to Hewlett (DGDGBE) • George Barbazan (DGDGBD) • Amelia (DGDGCD) • Will the Circle Be Unbroken (DADF#AD) • more.
00000224 Book/CD Pack $19.95

ARRANGING FOR OPEN GUITAR TUNINGS
By Dorian Michael
This book/CD pack teaches intermediate-level guitarists how to choose an appropriate tuning for a song, develop an arrangement, and solve any problems that may arise while turning a melody into a guitar piece to play and enjoy.
00000313 Book/CD Pack $19.95

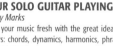

ROCK RHYTHM GUITAR
by Dave Celentano
This helpful book/CD pack cuts out all the confusing technical talk and just gives guitarists the essential tools to get them playing. With Celentano's tips, anyone can build a solid foundation of basic skills to play almost any rhythm guitar style. The exercises and examples are on the CD, in order of difficulty, so players can master new techniques, then move on to more challenging material.
00000274 Book/CD Pack $17.95

SCALES AND MODES IN THE BEGINNING
by Ron Middlebrook
The most comprehensive and complete scale book written especially for the guitar. Chapers include: Fretboard Visualization • Scale Terminology • Scales and Modes • and a Scale to Chord Guide.
00000010 ....$11.95

SLIDE GUITAR AND OPEN TUNINGS
by Doug Cox
Explores the basics of open tunings and slide guitar for the intermediate player, including licks, chords, songs and patterns. This is not just a repertoire book, but rather an approach for guitarists to jam with others, invent their own songs, and understand how to find their way around open tunings with and without a slide. The accompanying CD features 37 tracks.
00000243 Book/CD Pack $17.95

SPEED METAL
by Dave Celentano
In an attempt to teach the aspiring rock guitarist how to pick faster and play more melodically, Dave Celentano uses heavy metal neo-classical styles from Paganini and Bach to rock in this great book/CD pack. The book is structured to take the player through the examples in order of difficulty.
00000261 Book/CD Pack $17.95

25 WAYS TO IMPROVE YOUR SOLO GUITAR PLAYING
by Jay Marks
Keep your music fresh with the great ideas in this new book! Covers: chords, dynamics, harmonics, phrasing, intros & endings and more!
00000323 Book/CD Pack $19.95

Centerstream Publishing, LLC
P.O Box 17878 - Anaheim Hills, CA 92817
P/Fax (714)-779-9390 - Email: Centerstream@aol.com
Website: www.centerstream-usa.com